salmonpoetry

Publishing Irish & International
Poetry Since 1981

ALSO BY KEVIN HIGGINS

The Boy with No Face
(Salmon Poetry, 2005)

Time Gentlemen, Please
(Salmon Poetry, 2008)

Frightening New Furniture
(Salmon Poetry, 2010)

Mentioning the War: Essays & Reviews 1999-2011
(Salmon Poetry, 2012)

The Ghost in the Lobby
(Salmon Poetry, 2014)

Song of Songs 2.0: New & Selected Poems
(Salmon Poetry, 2017)

the arts council an chomhairle ealaíon

funding literature
artscouncil.ie

Sex and Death at Merlin Park Hospital

KEVIN HIGGINS

Published in 2019 by
Salmon Poetry
Cliffs of Moher, County Clare, Ireland
Website: www.salmonpoetry.com
Email: info@salmonpoetry.com

ISBN 978-1-912561-72-8

Cover Artwork: © Simon Campbell | Dreamstime.com
Cover Design & Typesetting: *Siobhán Hutson*

Printed in Ireland by Sprint Print

*Salmon Poetry gratefully acknowledges the support of
The Arts Council / An Chomhairle Ealaíon*

Contents

One – Sex and Death

Two – My View of Things

Three – World Festival of Literary Intercourse

One
Sex and Death

Sarcoid Years

after Gunter Eich

Sarcoid hours, the big blue dressing gown
your flag flapping about the town hall of you.
Your dream is a man running for a bus
and catching neither it nor his breath.
One o'clock is a book fallen open on your chest;
two is the cat nagging briefly at the door
then giving up.

Sarcoid days, twelve pills
on a Saturday. Last month's calendar
on the wardrobe door,
here where it's permanently before.
You clamber from the pit
of your weekly coma, coughing up chalk.
At the stethoscope your lungs are autumn
leaves under old brown slippers.

Sarcoid years, your alarm wakes
the tiny bird outside,
the one your cat's been trying to assassinate.
White phlegm indiscreetly into a hanky.
Calcium depositing itself here, there.
You are a developing bald patch
that spends alcohol free weekends
avoiding direct sunlight.
A bitten finger nail over and over again
telling a room this story's name.

Someday I'll Love Kweeveen O'Higgeen[*]

after Ocean Vuong

Kweeveen, time to start screaming.
The elevator has reached its basement destination;
when the door opens you'll see it's taken you
to the place of fire. Be suitably terrified.
Though you yelp your protests to the contrary,
your t-shirt is only your t-shirt until you start
using it as a loin-cloth. Like how the ocular prosthesis
won't remember how it once made sloppy
love to your eye's now sadly vacant socket
however often you kiss its roundness and tell it
it's not the miniature billiard ball it
imagines itself to be. Kweeveen,
have you put your new batteries in yet
and taken your first fist
load of medication? The most picturesque
bit of your lung is where the shadow
of your mother's cigarette smoke falls.
Worry yourself horrible
all the sweaty red night. Call it *oblivion*
write it down here and you
will reach it soon as the ink fades
and no one can be bothered decoding
what it was you were chirping on about.
Here's the day you took your dog to the vet
to have it shot. Drive through empty
streets shouting for joy and hope yours is not
an ejector seat remotely controlled
by your mutt's faithfully departed soul.
Here's the woman whose legs
are wide enough to gather
your enormous personality. And here
the moment before the burglar
you know is coming tonight
when you still see the lava lamp
between her thighs. How you use it
to guide Boeing 747s in to land.

You have asked for another cup of tea
and been given a mouth with which to drink it.
Sit there shaking with fear, that sound you hear
in the cupboard is the people who live in there
trying to die sooner. The least hideous
part of your body is all they want to eat
before they go. Just lie there and try
to forget you were ever alive.
Here's the room with everyone in it
but you. You passing through your friends
like a Cà Ri Gà chicken curry stew.
Here's a bicycle with one wheel missing
and a u-lock with no key
to stop you ever again trying
to cycle it rush hour
and have the entire city shake
its fist in your direction. And, yes, here's your coffin
sailing comfortably into the incinerator
so airy and spacious, I promise, you will wake
& mistake your skin for bacon
crackling in all your Sunday morning pans.

* Kweeveen O'Higgeen is the phonetic version of Caoimhín Ó hUiginn
which is Gaelic for Kevin Higgins

A Reckoning

after Christina Rosetti

My lungs are an accordion fallen out of tune
playing an air I've grown too used to.
Pour me tall glass after tall glass of summer sea air;
let me gulp them down with sliced strawberries.
My lungs belong in a shop
that sells second-hand bagpipes to the gullible.
May the cigarette smoke and diesel fumes of others
(and the mould and stress I brought to the table myself)
all be detained in the lamp-lit interrogation room
I'm building without planning permission
at the bottom of the garden.

My lungs are two talentless divas
competing with each other for newspaper headlines.
May everyone be arrested without warrant
and made plead.
Because the bill for my life is on the mat.
My lungs are rooms in which the yellow
wallpaper is slowly falling down.
My hates have come to get me
and are busy printing the word guilty on every
piece of paper they can find.

Sex and Death at the
Merlin Park Infusion Unit

after Saul Bellow

Blood pressure *okay*.
Temperature taken by a bit of plastic
she stuck in my ear,
the nurse straps a bag of magic
to my still relatively obliging vein.

Around me a room littered
with the even worse.
The mould of the grave
already about their faces.
Any month now they'll be served
to the maggot nurturing earth.

The look of them makes me want
to throw my arms –
while they still have flesh– around
every cubic centimetre of my wife;
the nurse with her firm fingers and soft eyes;
her more sombre colleague
who asked me just then
how my water-works have been;
even the bus-driver
who brought me here;
and my next-door neighbour
who was putting his bins out
as I was leaving the house;

to make wild
and inappropriate
love to the whole world.

The Medicines

after Thomas Hardy

This is the stuff no one likes
    And neither do I;
When the white pill tumbles
    Down the back of the settee,
And the cat leaps after it like a goalkeeper
    Failing to save a penalty
In the 1974 World Cup Final.
    And I fish its whiteness
From the depths, and while I'm there
    Find another one.

This is the yellow pill that prevents me
    Throwing up on people,
Except when absolutely necessary,
    And this is the orange pill
That stalls my hydrochloric acid
    When it tries to ruin my cup of tea,
And this is the green pill that helps me
    Stop killing people,
Except when absolutely necessary,
    And this is the clear bag of liquid
They drip into my arm every eight weeks,
    Which makes me want to have sex with everyone,
Even the Minister for European Affairs,
    Who my wife insists
Is too young for me anyway.

Prayer To The Absolute Dark

Forget, if you can,
most ungracious mind of burning hydrogen
never has it been known
that anyone who sought refuge in you,
implored your help down the telephone
you never answer,
or by pleading letter
sought your intervention
was ever aided.
Inspired by this matchless absenteeism,
I soar into your blackness.
Oh great impure one,
your mouth empty even of curses
before you I cower,
shamefaced and ragged
child of yours;
Mother, Father gas
made flesh,
despise my petitions,
as they should be
despised. In your
inclemency ignore
and answer me with
silent hymns
to the bacteria that must
victoriously consume
even the firmest, most perfect
belly.

Intimacy Revisited

Thirty years late, the couple who didn't make it.
We summit like the two Koreas
over French toast, Eggs Benedict.

And the first pot of tea still in play
we're already on my recent
explosive digestive episode;
seeing the humorous side of your
constipation, piles, and thoughts
about death. Given your love

of gardening, you like the idea of
a woodland burial,
not the sort serial killers
sometimes arrange
but those currently on offer
at a slightly too high price
from East Sussex County Council.

You want, you say, maggots
and worms to consume your flesh,
though hopefully not before we've
finished eating. I say I'm thinking
of donating my private parts
to The Museum of the Late Twentieth Century.

You reply that you always thought they'd look nice
safely skewered behind glass somewhere
people could bring their families on a Saturday
and examine them, from an
irretrievable distance.

For Cynthia

after Sextus Propertius

So put on your oilskins before you get
into bed or you'll feel all over you
the rain I bring everywhere with me.
Our talk is now mostly spittle. And we'll
have more subsiding flesh to show
each other come morning. We
have much to hide. Our bodies
are Wibbly Wobbly Wonders
melting in the sun. Before
they pass a law against it
let's have a festival of making do
with each other. For the daylight will soon
sneak in like an enemy agent.
Daylight without mercy or an off-switch.

Susan

after Andre Breton

Your hair is a wide brown meadow
through which the wind has just begun
to whisper the word winter.
Your eyebrows are caterpillars
perpetually on the verge of
moving off in opposite directions.
Your ears, two appropriately placed
question marks.
Your eyes are the calm surface of Lochs
in the Scottish Highlands which many
have sunk to the bottom of.
Cold days your right nostril
is a summer waterfall;
your left an angry traffic jam
on a crooked medieval street.
Your face is the sun coming up
over a Huguenot district.
Your lips are the Cote d'Azur in September.
Your teeth are monuments
to an actually existing utopia.
Your tongue is golden butter
insinuating itself into a hot pancake.
Your wrists and ankles
are engineering projects whose failure
led to a public inquiry that's expected
to go on forever.
Your belly-button, the permanently blocked keyhole
in a door with a sign on it that says
Ancient History.
Your most intimate bit is a nectarine
with a bite taken out of it.
Your toes are ten premature baby squirrels
that have tumbled blind and pink
to Earth.

Advice To A Modern Odysseus

after Homer

Spend hours convincing yourself the object of your lust
is the sort who takes milk in her Bovril and probably
eats cold Brussels sprouts by the basin load;
though even if she did, you know
it wouldn't matter in the least.

When you think of texting her,
employ local youths to tie you
to the nearest available electric fence
and leave you there. When
you eventually wriggle free

and still can't stop picturing her
pay your neighbours – the entire street –
in advance to arrange an orchestra
of chainsaws to block out
any possibility of her.

Join the Workers Revolutionary Party –
Lower Salthill branch – and spend
the next fifteen years racing about the place, saying the words
hegemonic, neoliberal, neo-colonialist
until no one anywhere will talk to you.

And when even this fails to kill your want
ask a kindly nun to drive a forklift truck
angrily over first your left
then your right foot.

When you come round in hospital
still muttering her name,
become a small time religious fanatic
and spend your evenings wisely
going door to door flogging
your own personal Jesus or Satan.

Behind the wife's back,
smuggle yourself in a taxi to the vet –
bringing the cat along for moral support –
and beg him to apply his trusty wire cutter
to your troublesome bit.

And when he refuses, publicly volunteer
to unblock free of charge other people's sewers
(any time of the day or night)
to remind your nostrils what everything
in the end turns into.

Yes, but also: mid-life story

I'm a Metro station outside which
men sell stolen cigarettes,
but I am also French onion soup
and L'Escargot eaten outside
on an August evening.

I am a family mausoleum
unvisited in decades,
but I am also pictures
of bright flowers and half naked women
dreamt onto a museum wall
by Gustav Klimt.

I am my trousers falling
down, due to ongoing
unexplained belly wasting;
but I am also the perfect dinner
our last night in Paris.

I am a grand piano discovering
it has eighty eight keys, all desperate
to be let sing,
only three of which have ever
been played before.

I am dead meat
with fingers all over it
bringing the blood back.

I am a formerly swollen
testicle which now must be approached
gently by a hand cloaked
in a pink fur glove.

I am the coming winter, yes.
But I am also not one but two
chocolate éclairs for breakfast.

Spring Day

after Rilke

Angel of ruin, it's time. The winter was too short.
Throw now your red shadow across the sky
and let the wind strip the beach of sand.

Let the first grapes turn to vinegar on the vine,
allow them enough bitter northern nights
to drag them to imperfection and coax
the final sourness to the top of your glass.

Who now has a bed to sleep in will not have one.
Who is together now will be put asunder,
will waken to the thing heaving beside her in the bed
and wander down motorways in her nightclothes
muttering at the traffic, watching new blooms hurry
south to keep their appointment with molten tarmac.

The Allegations Against You

after Brendan Behan

This committee finds, in your absence,
that you and your then girlfriend did conspire
together by your vigorousness to disable
a perfectly innocent settee.

We have in our hands a statement –
signed by said settee – which it took us
most of a week and several notebooks to construct.

Though we say so ourselves, our final edit
clarifies your guilt and is a definite
improvement on earlier drafts.

This has been a harrowing process
and everyone involved is exhausted,
especially the settee which, its psychiatrist says,
may never recover from what you two did to it.

Additions to your charge sheet include
that you did, on two occasions, take money
that was legitimately yours from under
one of the victim's cushions.

And that, on April the sixth nineteen ninety four,
you had for dinner two deceased
peanut M & Ms that had been happily
minding their own business down the back
of the violated settee, without seeking,
as you are legally required to, the settee's
written permission.

These most serious accusations will hang
about you like a dead fish under the floorboards
that only you can smell.

Until the hippopotamus, Truth,
rises from the river as it must.
By which time, no matter, you'll belong to us.

What I'm Prepared To Tell You

after Gunter Eich

This is my former shoe.
This is the book I'm not reading
at the moment. This is a picture of us
on honeymoon in Russia.

That Champagne cork on the mantelpiece
is of no particular significance.
The toy monkey beside it has no name
but keeps me company
when needs be.

The jar of beetroot in the fridge
I'm meant to eat
to counteract the side effects.
But not right now. The cat in the photograph
has been ten years
buried at the bottom of the garden.

The two light fixtures
either side of the fireplace
have never worked,
and I don't plan
to interfere with that
at this late stage.

The tiny wooden dolphin
on top of the bookcase,
we got in Birmingham, 1973
where child me
used to play rebel tunes
on the accordion.

About the toy Kalashnikov
perched discreetly in the corner,
the less said the better.

That cabinet door with the Wolfgang
Amadeus Mozart puppet dangling
from its handle, must be opened
under no circumstances whatsoever.

Several of the people in that far photograph
are no longer with us,
though not all of them
are, strictly speaking,
yet dead. Everything here
is exactly as it seems.

Ciúnas/Quiet

after Camillo Sbarbero

Ciúnas, sad person, these are the great
days when one must speak without whining.
The children of the long political sleep forced awake.
Like a vine heavy with grapes in peak season
laughing at its own potential riches,
I don't think I shall die again
and now know I did not die before.

Walking the public squares together again,
everyone clicking our picture,
I am there with you even when
three hundred miles away
on enforced holiday,
or home unable to get up for
lack of the necessary breath.
I am drawn to the recognised face
in the crowd, checking itself
in the shop window,
stunned to find itself here again.

At the pinnacle of a familiar song
sung anew, or the glimpse on a passing
TV screen of a pale boy being
what I once was, tears,
and my eyes relit with old light.
Because the permafrost I thought my lot
gives way, and the Earth shifts as it must,
I am like an old loudspeaker with a new battery
switched on after years in the garden shed.

Back there, I must not go,
as there's nothing but vacated spiders' webs
and the ruins of lamps and lawnmowers.

Put Me Back

after Vasko Popa

(i)

Put me back in that room
where I first learned to hate
you, though I didn't yet know
the full extent of you,
and you weren't yet
what you've become.

All you had to do
was open that hole
into which you now,
and with such style,
have a bespoke JCB
shovel tiramisu

and start blowing out
sounds, and in my thoughts
I was hacking off
your fingers with the chisel
we kept in the boiler house,
the one Mother left me in her will,
and which I retain, just in case.

The mistake you made:
reminding me you still exist;
that's what's come between us.

(ii)

Put me back in that room
with my new clock radio for Christmas.

The brown clock radio that brought
the world in, mornings before school.

The brown clock radio in which
the IRA almost exploded Maggie.

My brown clock radio in which
three hundred and sixty four days later,
the miners eventually lost.

Put me back in that room
and let me, one last time,
hug that brown clock radio, I knew
wasn't telling me the whole truth.

(iii)

Listen,
while I work out a new way
to erase you.

Relieve yourself of your dinner jacket.
Sit back, and drink this.

I've known you since I was so high,
and you'd already spent four
centuries counting money
you call yours.

Consult the mouldy old file
your people kept on me. You'll find
I spent more than a decade trying
to kill you, though I wouldn't have known
you if you leapt naked through
my parents' living room window.

Loosen that tie before it
prematurely garrottes you, and try
your latest lie out on me.

(iv)

Stop trying to sell me
a genetically modified cat
to chase the genetically perfected hamster
you sold me yesterday

across the carpet you say
needs replacing;

or a kidney that once belonged to
a woman who had an unfortunate accident
at a T junction near Macclessfield;

or a drone I could use
to terminate you.

(v)

No, I'm not interested in buying back
the hair that came out in the brush,
when I dutifully gobbled that last batch
of medication you flogged me.

No, I won't be leasing back from you
my old knees
to again wear them out
walking the streets against you.

I won't be remortgaging
this sad, sagging thing
I rest on the sofa
you sold me earlier.

Put me back in that room,
where I didn't know the half of you.

(vi)

Put me back in that room,
where there was still some chance
you were a game
I was playing with myself in my head.

Let that brown clock radio again
soothe me safely back to sleep.

The Great News

after Eugenio Montale & Karl Marx

So many mornings I woke hoping
to find you there
and when there was no sign
how many times
I clicked on that brown clock-radio
praying to hear tell of you.
The blood rising at every fuzzy mention
of your name. The thought of you
strutting into town to clean
things up with your Guillotine
wiped away crazy aunts
shouting my name over the fence,
the bastards in my Latin class,
and the girls who kept saying nyet.
So many moments you seemed about
to emerge from the crowd:
Father Burke Park, Chinatown, Trafalgar Square.
But you kept not quite making it.

In the finish I had to sit
at the desk I could by then
afford to buy myself
and sign the decree banning
utterance of your name.

Now, thirty years late
you and your shadow opposite
are both everywhere
abolishing the colour grey,
swaggering off trains,
climbing out of computers
and television sets
wearing masks I recognise.
Now to rummage in the closet
under the stairs and see where mine got to;
make it fit an altogether
fatter head than it was intended for.

Coalition of The Disappointed

We the undersigned wish to register
with you, the good people of the internet,
our disappointment
that our one time mentor-therapist-guru
with whom we have fallen
totally out of love,
appears to be dying
more slowly
than we the undersigned
would like,

Unmentionable now in the company
women of our status aspire to keep
he once put us standing on high stages,
adjusted microphones for us,
got our names in the relevant
provincial newspapers,
and said them
over and over again
on sociable media
until it became a bit embarrassing
to be honest or, even,
dishonest,
and we could do nothing
but lust
after the sound of ourselves.

Now all he does is stink up
our timelines with quips
about Marie Antoinette being
just as much victim of the patriarchy
as Meghan Markle;
and how the term "political veganism"
makes him long to tear
a rump steak
off the nearest available cow
and race naked around the Albuquerque
Red and Green VegFest
eating it.

Such rude levity is commendable
when one's breaking down the door
but not when one's trying to say inside the room
and make one's way to nod and silently sympathise
with the Minister for Culture and Heritage
on her recent bank loan faux pas.

After his update last week
we must move his last breath
from the "impending" to at least
the "medium-term-aspiration" section;
can't help but fret this good news
might be the start of a disastrous
long term recovery on his part,
like that of the Soviet Army
at Stalingrad. An eventuality
which could, if things went wrong,
or, even, right,
lead to ladies of our disposition
and quality
being made dine
on Cyanide.

Yours sincerely,

Poet of page and stage Eiléan Ní Faitíos,
Our Lady of the Sorrowful Status Updates,
The Third World Liberation Wing of Galway Lawn Tennis Club,
Irish Nee Haircut,
Poet and Critic Dr. Silica Tradeup

Two

My View of Things

When I Wasn't Yet

after Holderlin

When I wasn't yet a man
the one with giant dusty white wings
would pretend to rescue me
from no one to play soccer with
and nothing on the television
my sisters monopolised anyway.

And we'd kick a ball back and forth
among the dock leaves and thistles
secure in our tornness.

And hurricanes from below,
like a line of baby devils
being winded by their mother
sprang up and cheered us on.

Of all his devils
I was his least favourite.
That faithless malignancy,
I wish you could know
how in my guts I hated
that I tried to pretend he existed.

I knew him to be no better
than any of the rest of them,
understood the wasps coming out of their nest
but never the words with which men
and women always acquit themselves.

Nettles were my professors,
tone deaf interlopers,
and I learned to despise
among the strange things that grew wild there.

For I grew up in the arms of briars.

The Day Bowie Died

after Frank O'Hara

Somewhere else,

Lulu is blowing morning kisses
to the mirror, looking forward to another day
of making increasingly thin hay
out of having once been married to a Bee Gee.

Gary Barlow is furiously trying to get through
to his accountant.

Mick Hucknall is rediscovering
Buddhism, and watching a fox
be torn to small morsels by hounds.

Cliff Richard is madly practising
his dance moves, and thinking about maybe
later playing some tennis.

Kanye West is not being disposed of
in a septic tank in one of the less
salubrious parts of Roscommon.

Noel Gallagher is tragically
waking up alive, and babbling
about how Jeremy Corbyn is a
communist, fascist, Cistercian,
or some other word he recently learned
to (sort of) pronounce.

This day that began with the red
head of our cat Ziggy
announcing itself against
the bedroom door.

After the terrible events earlier

Days like this, our very way of life
(and death) under attack we realise
we are in this together: your pet assassin, Fang,
and the mouse whose corpse
she dumped on the doorstep this morning;

the sunlit girl playing hopscotch
in the school playground, and the man
across the road watching her intently
and sweating small waterfalls into
his vastly experienced cheap grey overcoat;

the widow in the dress she'll wear
in her own coffin and the funeral director
his head tilted to indicate
how sad he is to be taking the last of her money;

the aid agency official on an all-expenses
paid trip to Phnom Penh
and the escort struggling for her breath
under his shuddering bulk;

the senile old dear putting out her budgie, Harry,
for the night and the burglar who's coming
to cave her skull in with a hatchet;

the supermarket majority shareholder
looking out his hotel window
at the moon over Lake Geneva
and the checkout assistant with holes in both her shoes
whose soul he quietly owns.

Though rest assured
tomorrow, or the day after,
normal will be back to its British best
every paw for its grabbing,
infected self.

Until the next outbreak
of "terrible", "sick", "depraved",
when we'll be temporarily
in this (whatever this is)
together again.

In The White Man's Clinic

A grand piano plays itself
on a giant Chinese rug
in a foyer so vast I once went there
by mistake, hoping
to catch a long haul flight
to Melbourne via Abu Dhabi.

Instead found myself in a glass palace
where surgeons do things
no one thought possible
and which, in the end, weren't;

in the process making sad intestines sing
like water damaged concert violins,
lungs hoot like ruined tubas
in a building designed to mature
into a hotel, when it fails as a hospital
for those who can afford to die
during office hours.

Sold

The window I once climbed in.
The room where I learned my Latin.
The telephone that was twice cut off.
The hallway light that was always on.
The kettle I was constantly boiling.
The window by which our Christmas tree stood.
The bathroom the President of Ireland once used.
The bedroom in which a student unsuccessfully slit her wrists.
The doorbell the Socialists rang to summon me.
The letter box my school reports came in through.
The front door I still have a key to.
The room I saw her die in.

Heavy Clogs

I'm the local schoolmistress
who worked hard to know
the zilch I knew about this.

I'm the Department Inspector
who remembered
the questions not to ask.

I'm the concerned citizen who never
heard their heavy clogs go,
by forced marches, up the Dublin Road.

I'm the editor of the Tuam Herald,
who talked instead about
the Pope's visit.

I'm the Government Minister whose pink skull
baldly admired the particular yellow
of the roses by the newly whitewashed wall,
and thanked the nuns for their work.

I'm the County Councillor concerned
about the cost to the ratepayer
— per skeleton — of piling that many small ones
of whom no one had ever heard

into a disused hole in the ground
— one big concrete sarcophagus —
no one knew anything about.

Leader of Irish Government Speaks Against Hyperbole

after William Shakespeare

There has been much hyperbolic comment of late
about the admittedly rather sad case of a man
who had his new corneas removed
by two blokes from Lithuania
or Neilstown (somewhere like that)
because he fell behind with the payments.

I had one of my interns watch
the video of the action those men took
to recover that part of his eyes a judge
ruled belonged to the company
on whose behalf they were acting,
and though the defaulter – I mean man – in question
has my sympathy, particularly regarding
the apparent lack of anaesthetic,
think about it this way:

every time you see one of those
click bait headlines about a tragic
granny who had her new heart ripped
back out and the papery old one reinstalled
by a team of cut-price cardiologists
appointed by an esteemed
judge whose daddy bought him a law degree,
because she spent all her pension on scratch cards,
it's an example of the market
and rule of law weaving their magic,
as Adam Smith intended.

To let old ladies we all know, and sympathise with,
off paying for their new tickers
when they have insufficient funds to meet
the direct debit would be the ruin
of our financial institutions
and put us as a country in breach
of the rules of both the World Trade Organisation
and European Court of Justice.

So, next time you read about a child
with profligate parents who this Christmas was made hand
a transplanted kidney back
to its rightful owners, the bank of wherever;
remember, it's just
our free economy doing shit it must.

What Did The Politician Get His Wife?

after Bertolt Brecht

And what did she get, the girlfriend,
from the student union meeting
at which he rose to his feet
and realised he could speak?
From that meeting she got
the Snickers bar he forgot to eat
so busy was he watching them listen;
and that speech, unabridged,
every other night for thirty five years.

And what did she get, his new wife,
from the time he first used a party
conference microphone to agree with both sides?
Those okay with the Muslims/Mexicans/Gypsies being here,
and those who want them kept over there.
From that microphone she took away their
invitation to dine with the Deputy Mayor
and his not new wife.

And what did she get, his no longer new wife,
when, at the second attempt,
he won that seat on the City Council?
From his election she got to drink Pinot Noir
and go swimming in their private club
with the no-so-new wives
of those who got the contracts
to make the paving stones and install
the pay-and-display ticket machines
during his years as Chairman
of the relevant committee.

And what did she get, his well-maintained wife,
the night he was elected to the big shiny
parliament? From that night she took away
an architect to re-design their new three storey pad
in the priciest possible part of the capital,
and an article about herself
in the Daily Express lifestyle pages.

And what did she get, the no longer new MP's
no longer new wife, the morning
they made him Minister?
That morning she got to go horse riding
with the Leader of the House of Lords'
fourth (or fifth) wife.

And what did she get, the no longer new
Cabinet Minister's wife, the night the landslide
made him Prime Minister? That night
she got to hold to her breast
invitations to break foie gras
with the Sultan of Brunei, the President of China;
and the chance to write husband's speech
announcing the crackdown on beggars
who accost hard working
families who stop to ask for directions
en route to the nearest funeral parlour.

And what did she get, the ex-Prime Minister's
no longer new wife, from all the depleted uranium shells
he had dropped during the Battle of Basra, all the soldiers
he sent to meet improvised explosive
devices in far Mesopotamia in the hope
of getting rid of something bigger
than the beggars and prostitutes
at King's Cross. From these she got
white night terrors
of him on trial for all their crimes,
and the desire to never again
look out the front window of their fine
Connaught Square house
at the tree from which, it's said,
they used to once string
traitors.

Don't Stop Repealing

after Journey

In the interests of the coming equality,
of which everyone is now theoretically
in favour, the mahogany dining tables of Taylors' Hill
must be immediately confiscated; the wood used
to fashion a makeshift grand piano
for every asylum seeker child in the city.

All marble staircases will be yanked out,
like massive teeth, and delivered
to the nearest band of traveller children
to do with as they wish.

Former Senators, with fully paid-up
Galway Golf Club memberships,
must be auctioned off to buy
T-bone steaks for seasonally unemployed
fish factory hands.

To further redress the class balance,
it will be compulsory
for the Armed Response Unit to legally remove
by shooting as many times as necessary
any auctioneers or Papal Nuncios
seen acting suspiciously outside
the kebab shop.

Property developers of all genders,
races, and sexual orientations who purchase
half finished apartment blocks
for the very heaven of just watching
the price rise, will be taken forcibly

in the back of an obliging HiAce
to the nearest available handball alley,
where they'll be given fifty strokes
across each cheek
by some mad eejit with a grudge.

Ireland, May 26th, 2018

SJW from Horse Hair Hill

after Erich Fried

Because her vertebrae
are all exactly where they're supposed to be.
Because she never raises her voice when
refuting what the last speaker said.
Because she has no need of deodorant.
Because she is strong enough to go on living
long after the regime from whose womb
she sprang, already speaking
perfectly formed sentences,
has either died or renewed itself,
and whoever names streets
after people like her
has already named several after her;
the regime she both hates
for what it does to people
who can't speak
perfectly formed sentences
and loves for paying her to talk
words on their behalf
without getting personal like you
insist on doing.

Because her vertebrae
are all marked present and correct
and yours are twisted with jealousy and pain
Because she is above shouting
at the likes of you
Because she has no need of deodorant
but is the deodorant regimes
old and new occasionally need
to prove there is no smell –
except the one you bring to the table –
and nothing to shout about here.

My View of Things

after Edwin Morgan

What I love about lateness is the hope
I might get to slip off home before you turn up.
What I hate about punctuality is always getting there
in time to chat before you leave.
What I love about angle-closure glaucoma
is not seeing you
when you're standing right in front of me.
What I hate about comebacks
is the possibility you'll have one.
What I love about impotence is the sight
of you jiggling your bits at me in the hope I might
review your book/pretend to like your poetry/remember
your name, and it having no effect whatsoever.
What I love about my chronic lung condition
is the hours of enforced sleep during which I can dream
of a world in which I've never heard of you.
What I love about going slowly deaf
is not being able to hear the television.
What I love about nuclear holocaust
is the TV studio, in which those three men
are agreeing with each other, will no longer exist.
What I love about Crohn's disease
is the hours I spend on the toilet,
during which I miss comedy panel shows
in which Alan Davies talks to Alan Davies
about Alan Davies. What I love about your likeable face
is my ability, most days, to see past it.
What I hate about you wondering why Trump won
is your failure to look in the mirror.
What I love about memory is remembering
your rhetorical question:
How many Palestinian publishers are there?
What I love about dementia is the chance to forget
you once, very briefly, existed.

Let Me Tell You About Them

The teenagers we shot yesterday
were shot responsibly through the eye
with plain-speaking dum-dum bullets,
manufactured in Fife, or taken down
with SR 25 sniper rifles flown
heroically in from Orange County.
Many of these so-called protestors
specifically arranged to be shot in the back,
just to make us look bad.

The gas canisters our people threw
were entirely rational, and legal,
like the Boer firestorm the kaffirs
brought down on themselves at Sharpeville,
or the best-of-British ambush
that rubbish walked into at Derry.

The one rogue canister which lost
its mind and finished up in a tent
beside an eight month old baby,
who, sadly, also expired, is currently under investigation
and expects to be cleared of all wrong doing,
unlike the baby who we've already found guilty.

There is no such thing as Palestinians.
Just some Arabs who used to live here
and think they still do.
The keys they wave in the air
no longer open any doors.
They are a rumour you foolishly believed,
now we've moved our eternal capital
to what used to be
their front room.

17-5-2018

The Truth Behind the Wire

Kindly disregard the attention seeking cries of the few.
They are child actors being given scripts by liberals.
Most of the young people there are delighted with
what we're doing. There is no policy
of separation from parents. It's just
if you're going to process the mamas
and papas, you've gotta take
the bambinos away.
The wire we put around them,
for their own safety, isn't even barbed.
In there, we help kids go to school;
even give them haircuts
with our giant – and deadly
accurate – Immigration
and Customs Enforcement scissors.

This is the exact opposite of cages.
Despite the headlines,
no one has been gassed.
There are, and never have been,
no concentration camps.
These children are in temporary custody;
playing video games
and soccer; getting two snacks
a day and lots of sleep
under their resplendent thermal blankets.
The chain-link fencing
we've used to divide into bedrooms
the building we're warehousing them in
is entirely incidental.

Almost none of the adolescents in our possession
have, as of yet, been turned
into bespoke hat-stands
and raffled off to the dissatisfied wives
of Texan cattle-hands.

And we have, as of today, no plans
to use the hindquarters of the small ones
to fashion a new face for
Rupert Murdoch.

Beige Heterosexuals

after Jameson Fitzpatrick

Oppression is a brown woman,
who used to be beige and called
Gerald, until she discovered it
an unfortunate name for a girl,
taking up no seats on the bus
because she prefers to travel
in the luggage compartment,
despite always buying
at least three tickets.

It is also my both telling you,
and yet not telling you, how she looked
when she emerged with the rest of the luggage
a little less brown than when she dived in there
but, so far as we could tell, still heterosexual
and no longer named anything like Gerald.

Oppression is also her body's distance,
socially and physically, from the lavatory
-which is no great shakes anyway —
on this bus she is taking from
Ballina and I am taking
from Sligo. And how

my finding her bladder control,
in which I must put my faith, impressive
makes me no more likely to ask,
should her gaze meet mine,
why the fuck anyone would
choose to travel that way.

What I'm trying to say is distance
is the problem with formerly beige
heterosexual women
who choose to travel in luggage compartments.
I'm not one of them, so I can both write this poem
and at the same time
not write it.

Distance, because it offers
the possibility of her not being there
when the luggage is claimed;
that she may turn out
to be imaginary and never to have been
either beige or called Gerald.

Oppression is both me being unable
to find a place for my suitcase
because the luggage compartment's chuck full of
now brown heterosexual women
each of them originally called something like Gerald
—an unfortunate name for a girl—
and me later on denying these women's existence.

Internet Safety For Adults

When Her Majesty squiggles my law into effect,
it will be compulsory that every computer come
with a paedophile pre-installed.
Section four of the proposed legislation
will make it mandatory that said individual
only be activated when your child types
in his or her date of birth and a verifiable
I.D. card number which I, as Minister
for Children, will provide for each of them
free of charge. From this day forth your sons and daughters
will no longer have to haunt
local playgrounds in the hope of being accosted
by men enthusiastic to open
the all-encompassing grey coats
their type travel the land in.

Worry not, the frothing men (and occasional women)
the tech giants will, from now on, be compelled
to put inside every computer in the country
will be tested to ensure they have no interest in adults.
Obese chain-smoking blokes from near Stoke
and the sort of women whose implausibly
distended chests one notices
at post-nightclub bus-stops in Bishop's Stortford
will be in no danger whatsoever.

The people to whom we plan to introduce your children
have no appetite for mutton, or dry aged sirloin;
only eat choice cut spring lamb
done exquisitely rare.

from Things That Keep Tim Awake of A Winter's Night

Most of all, it's where
some men like to put their members.
Especially when it's into each other.

Though he doesn't think it sinful, exactly,
it creases that expanse of pinkness
known as his forehead to
think of them pushing their tenderest bit into
theologically questionable apertures.

Next thing they'll be poking it
through strangers' letter boxes; shoving
it up the exhaust pipes of cars
they're jealous they can't afford,
or through the cat flaps of old ladies
named Doris and Edith,
just for the thrill of putting it
somewhere new.

They'll be detained for questioning,
having been found apparently trying to squeeze it
through the key hole of their future
father-in-law's front door;
injure themselves by using it
to probe the entrance
to a nest of wasps, or forcing it
down the neck
of a bottle of Scotch whiskey
to see if it stings;

or they'll render it
unusable by ramming it
into a cold hearted
turboforce meat grinder
which will make of it a burger
no self-respecting evangelical
could – *praise Jesus!* –
ever knowingly eat.

Members of every shape and persuasion
gratuitously placed in harm's ravenous jaw,
things like this keep Tim wide eyed and frantic
past two, three, five past four…

Fixing The National Discourse

for an Doctúir Mary McAuliffe

When each adjective, noun, verb,
and swear word
has been put through the purifying machine
we're perfecting,
those found wanting
abolished by our all conquering delete button;
to safeguard our newfound purity
it will be compulsory for
urban district councils, kindergartens, universities
and non-gubernatorial organisations in receipt
of morbidly obese
public largesse to employ
a pair of performing jaws
from the better bit of town
as Language Ombudsperson
and General Controller of Talk,
to inform you when you're saying it wrong
and send the offending ex-words
down the U-bend
where they belong.

It will be an offence,
persecutable under law,
to us the 'k' word, the 'd' word,
or the 'r' word,
even in the privacy of one's own
mind, except for purposes of historical
study of the political and linguistic
degeneracy of the recent past.

Civil servants will be made read
enough Foucault so they never
inadvertently commit a hate crime
while typing the now traditional
letter of refusal in response to
applications for housing, health care,
welfare...

Furthermore, mention of Led Zeppelin
will heretofore be prefaced
with the health-warning:
quartet of toxic masculinity,
and use of the phrase *beautiful blue eyes*
accepted as proof of
closet membership of the Ku Klux Klan
by our new non-jury online courts.

As well as having
no effect whatsoever on actual
living, breathing inequality and hatred
for which it'll be business as usual;
these measures will help us attract
increased foreign direct investment into
our seething little country.

In five years,
ninety percent of you will be working
twelve jobs and paying twice
your monthly income to rent a shed
with a tin roof from the love-child
of Google and the ThyssenKrupp corporation
and be so grateful
you won't dare spit a nasty word
against anyone.

Refusal

after Les Murray

In as many languages as necessary:
nyet, nien, less chance
I'll click love on the latest post-
post-avant-garde patio you've addended
to the foundationless house of your theory,
than of a bull exiting a slaughterhouse's iron jaws
with his swaggering rump intact.

I'd rather tear out bits of my own liver
with an argumentative breadknife,
mash it into a paté and serve it
atop water biscuits to the next meeting
of your posh ladies' poetry semi-circle;
than listen to those who say hourly rosaries
to the Etruscan goddess, Mania
to be made tenured Chair of Thin, Fat, or Bald Studies,

when you open a mouth-load of exquisite
teeth to speak of the pink willy privilege
of discontinued West Virginia coalminers,
who have nothing better to do now
than sit on the porch all day,
blackening their hankies,
like aristocrats.

Anatomy of a Bomb scare

for Jacqueline Walker

Tasks such as this are typically implemented
on deniable mobile phones,
ordered by a raised eyebrow or nod
fourth or fifth floor
of an unpainted, concrete building,
about which no more can be said because,
for reasons obvious to both
The Guardian and the Daily Star – though they
choose different language to say
so – the security services never comment on
operational matters.

It's the unanimous advice of a committee
of twenty seven former Attorney Generals,
the Chair of the BBC board of governors, and all ex
Archbishops of Canterbury (living and dead)
that for reasons of national well being no record must be kept
of the twitchy eyebrow or official looking
nod of the head in question. Such things are done
by loyal servants of things as they must remain
when sending round Balaclavad policemen
(and women) might prove counterintuitive.

On rare occasions some independent maniac
in a top floor flat with hardly any windows
who generally speaking couldn't organise
a butt rub at a tantric sex party,
to which he'd never be invited anyway,
inspired by the sweaty ravings
of our Twitter bots which unlike Russia's
don't exist, miraculously manages to plant a bomb,
and as at Bologna, Dublin, Monaghan
puts a mass of concrete and angle-grinders asunder,
leaves jaw and shin bones separate
from the heads and legs to which they were
until seconds ago attached, there
in the foyer for some rank and file cop
to collect, bag and label;

or drives a box of nine inch nails
into what we consider politically expendable eyeballs
at five hundred kilometres per hour.
Such actions are a bonus
and we welcome their contribution
to our ongoing struggle,
though they're not officially sanctioned.

Mostly our task is to convince
people we don't exist,
except in the minds of pink eyed conspiracists;
to tend the fungus doubt
that the likes of you,
dear victim,
probably divide your Mondays
between subsidised yoga and phoning in threats
against yourself.

Listening Exercise

after John McDonnell

When you paint hatred on my garden wall
and front door, I will read your words
with great interest.

When you try to burn my house down
I will listen to what the flames are saying.

Every lie you tell against me
I'll help you spread
by earnestly, and in detail, answering your questions
about it over and over again.

When you burst through my living room door
with a chainsaw intended for me,
I'll pour you a nice cup of tea
and say: let's talk about this.

When the tumours come for me
I'll know their opinion must be taken
absolutely on board.

And when the beetles and bacilli
begin to consume me,
I'll realise I've long seen
their point of view.

Pity The Woman Made of Wood

Crowned temporary Empress
of this tragic bit of chipboard floating
off the northernmost coast
of what used to be Europe.

Open please your hearts, empty your heads
and pretend not to notice the predictable few
disfigured old bastards who operate her,
yanking the all too visible wires
that make her jaws clack
awkwardly up and down. Pity please
this woman made of wood
now she's too well understood
and gets all the kicks and expletives,
when she tries to speak about
anything other than the quarterly accounts.

Her back burdened and bent.
Respect please the enormity
of the pearls she must bear
about her splintering neck.
And don't be behind with the rent
or petition her to save you when you again
characteristically fail to save yourself.

When smoke curls black under your door
you can snore on unperturbed in your narrow little bed,
bought with a pay-day loan obtained – quite legally –
from a bloke reputed to give defaulters
cement flip-flops for Christmas, to take them safely
down one of the larger pipes that joyfully
pour shit into the River Styx.

But the woman made of wood
must at all costs avoid
unguarded flames for she would go up
like a cheap deckchair that picked the wrong
day to go sunbathing at Hiroshima.

Think of this, please, when bawling
your lucky human screams
as the fire arrives quite matter-of-fact
to oxidise you to a small hill of ashes
around what looks like
a collar bone. No such luck
for the woman made of wood.

The Great Repeal

"As it happens, personally I have always been in favour of fox hunting"

THERESA MAY

Furthermore,
when we abolish the political correctness gone mad
that is the Human Rights Act,
it will again be legal to strip and smear
Conservative parliamentary candidates
with animal fat and pursue them with hounds
through the Devon countryside
bank holiday Mondays; legal

to remove from your property
with a horse whip or, failing that, a cross bow
any Daily Mail journalists
you catch going through your bins;

legal to tie down and spread tuna fish oil all over
the Chairman (or Woman) of a FTSE 100 company
and leave the rest
to your expert team of feral cats;

legal to chase
with demented Alsatians
through Welwyn Garden City of a Wednesday
former rock journalists with nothing left
but their opinion of themselves;

legal in certain parts of East Sussex
to set starving greyhounds
on anyone you think resembles
a retired tennis player
or Mike Reed of the BBC;

legal again to hunt, using properly licensed rifles,
decayed intellectuals
with nothing now going on under
their formerly magnificent hair
on the anniversary of Professor Norman Stone's funeral;

legal once more to celebrate
St. George's Day by following
Pippa Middleton around Herefordshire with bulldogs
and a temperamental shotgun;

when the British people rise,
put the B back into Britain
and she once again rules
the itsy-bitsy waves
around the Isle of Wight, mate.
The waves around the Isle of Wight.

The Thing from Planet Gove

Its handshake is that of a slightly disreputable funeral director.
Its eyes those of an opinionated alligator
that sometimes reviews opera for the London Times.
Its mind is a free trade slaughterhouse, busy
making mincemeat, as cleanly as possible,
of other people's children, bony old parents
and the occasional small business person
who was just wrong place, wrong century.

But its regular appearances on TV impress
the sort of people who have sexual relations
with their cars. Or their neighbours
cars. The female it dreams of is
Rupert Murdoch's more withered sister
who lets it stand on its tippy-toes in a tutu
inherited from a former grandmother
who was briefly a dowager Duchess
until the unfortunate headlines
made her true position undeniable.

And it is written in Scripture
that at a time such as this
a thing such as this
would ascend to Earth and give us –
leaving god aside for the minute –
proof of Satan's existence.

What Put The Diamonds
In Your Owner's Wife's Ears?

after Bertolt Brecht

You clean collared columnists
should first help us fix the basic roof-over-head
dilemma, before penning your next sermon.

You shower, who preach *careful now*
and always know your own exact bank balance,
what is this *mature democracy* towards which you sweat?
Without a door I can safely lock behind me
to keep your pity at bay, *civilisation*
doesn't even begin.

First bring those of us who get by on Supermacs
each our own mahogany table and a big, silver knife
with which to cut the turkey and ham into manageable slices
(with a vegetarian option for those so afflicted)
and answer us this:

What put the diamonds in your owner's wife's ears?
Or the Prince Albert ring in her boyfriend's willy?
The fact you're in there polishing phrases
and we're out here in the undemocratic rain
which everyone – from the Primate of the Church of Ireland
to the Council for the Women of Consequence – agrees
must never be allowed land on you,

this is what keeps pinning diamonds
to your owner's wife's sad little lobes,
and puts the ring that winks up at her
in her boyfriend's knob.

The Minister for Loneliness

First day behind my hugely plausible new desk
I will begin making secret cash payments
in paper bags that smell of donuts
to all citizens – upstanding and not – on the strict
condition they sign this twelve page contract
agreeing to henceforth avoid the likes of you.

On my watch the only job you'll get
will be nights guarding the hugely valuable
glass and steel of an empty office block
in a city where no one wants to know you.

Romance, for you, will consist of regular visits
to the launderette in the hope
there's someone there to talk to.
But even the lip-sticked lady who sits there
most of most days, crocheting
tea cosies and sharing her arthritis,
will vamoose when she sees you coming.

I will make sure
you have no missed calls,
nothing in your in-box,
and get no letters, not even a curt epistle
from your soon-to-be ex-wife's solicitor.

You'll be a sparrow
chirping madly for a missing mate
long since safely
in the jaws of the cat
who answers to me.

Your existence will shrink until
you and your pet mosquito are the sole tenants
in an otherwise boarded up block that looks out
on the radiant windows
of those determined not to know you.

The Man Who Spoke Slogan

He was forever bursting through the doors
of occupied bathrooms, bellowing:
The whole world is watching.

When caught wearing his first wife's tights
he turned on the megaphone and began shouting:
Get your rosaries of our hosieries.

When Mayo suffered another catastrophic
one point All Ireland final loss,
he rode through Castlebar on his Harley-Davidson
singing loud as he could:
The workers have no county.

When he interrupted burglars about to make off
with his credit cards, lap-top,
phone, and hugely expensive watch,
he earnestly told them: *There are no illegal people,*
and they immediately went screaming
down the driveway.

When his second wife found him wedged
between the au pair's breasts, he told her:
He who has the youth has the future.

And when the students next door gratuitously chucked
yet another sweet-wrapper in his front
garden, he ran around it bollock-naked, roaring:
For the many, not the few. Build the wall!

Prologue

Back when there were still income tax and traffic lights.
When people still put things in microwave ovens
and ate them afterwards sat on what they used to call
sofas, while watching outtakes from The Apprentice
on that other, second-most-important
mid-twentieth century invention.

Back when there was still an internet
and people could access electricity
by just plugging in the kettle,
didn't have to stand under a rare tree
in all-too-frequent storm and hope for the worst.

Back when two small people spent
what would be their final years in a gorgeous
pre-World War Three house,
built on land that's now far beneath
an ocean there's no one around to name,

in which the bacteria and an occasional
three eyed fish nightly celebrate their victory.

Hoodied Bridget

after Bertolt Brecht & Kurt Weill

You've seen me doing my hours emptying clean
the ashtrays of third hand taxis cabs
and scrubbing hard with bleach their tainted back seats
before they're offered up again
to the god of whatever the market fetches
in a town the government has privately agreed
is to be discontinued, and wondered
what's with her smirk?

You've seen me doing my hours
in the two Euro shop and considered
offering me twenty quid
for a quick ride around the back
of the disused funeral parlour
next door. For you've no idea
what I am.

If you'd any sense
you'd wake screaming
every night in fear of me.
By the time you do
I'll be standing over you
and you'll still be wondering
what's with her smirk?

For there's a crowd coming behind me
carrying a flag you won't believe
you're seeing again
until you do.

You'll go red in the face like an old fool
about to choke to death during sex, and tell me
I'll have fries with that.
For you've no clue who I am.
You'll fumble for your wallet
and toss me a fifty Euro tip, and wonder,
one last time, what's with her
insufferable smirk?

For by then the ship
you thought would never come in
will have quietly docked
flying a flag you'll remember
from the history books.
Its contraband cargo
that will give us the metal to own
everything you think rightfully yours
being silently unloaded by others like me
made what they are
by years looking at the likes of you
poured into your waistcoat, believing in
the divine right of your money.

My pals will be here presently – knock knock –
with their methods of persuasion and
the flag they rescued from the dustbin
in which you tried to bury it.

First question they'll pop
when they see you tied up here
will be *toss him in the skip right now,*
or *lock him in the attic for later?*

Knock knock knock

Three

World Festival of
Literary Intercourse

Up with Clever Literature

after Roy Campbell

Enough of these who just strip back the wrapper
to lay bare the mould that's got into the marriage,
what clergy, journalist, and judge

are wearing under their frocks – who put in your face
the receipts – who exactly pays
for the Archbishop of Canterbury's

Buttercup panties. We want verses
that dress our beetle ridden corpses so thoroughly
in what look like peacock feathers,

no one would know we've been dead for years.
And, before that, metaphors that blind like a comb-over,
so successful the reader forgets the ham

beneath. The literature-appreciating public expect
men in casual jackets going up hills and realising
no one knows exactly what;

need to know how Queen Medbh
might have reacted to something you think
you read in the *I-Ching*
or *Eat, Love, Pray* while your temporal human form
was temporarily stuck on a broken down Southern Rail train.

Give us themes like these in metres preferred
by the Persians, or Charles the Twelfth of Latvia,
so Professors with banjaxed hair
can spend half a century working out
what it was you were getting at,

or, even, what you weren't.

Feral Hogs

after Mary Oliver

You do not have to be bad.
There is no granite law of biology, physics,
or chemistry that insists you must poke
your steaming snout into dinner plates and laps
not yours to investigate
for the possibility of nosh
or interspecies coitus.
Give me your list of humans
you found in the desert and tried to eat,
and I will give you mine.
All the while the universe continues to expand
or slowly implode. Physicists differ
and regularly have televised wrestling matches
over matters such as this.
All the while the ocean's temper rises
and occasionally abolishes
some island in the Pacific. But no matter.
All the while feral hogs like you drag
their bacon selves home.
However bigly you think of your self
history sizzles and spits like frying sausages,
takes you by the trotter
to your place in the butcher's shop of things.

Uncrease Your Forehead and Do Not Sweat

after Rupi Kaur

My recipe is this, Stepfather said
caressing his tumbler of whiskey,
as if it were a loaded shotgun:
go driving madly
up the slitheriest hills
on non-existent roads
in stolen Austin Allegros
with five tyres
one flatter than the other
to cottages from which the windows
have been torn,
like bad teeth
from infected gums
without delay or mercy, all in the one day,
in preparation for your arrival;
so the pigeons can fly
in and out freely
and peck from the plate
what would have been
your lunch, let gull
and crow fight their raucous duel over who
gets to make off with your glasses
and the loser take to its nest
in the far tree
your false teeth.
Lie then on that mattress
without springs.
Let what remains of the eiderdown
disintegrate all about you.
And accept it
when the universe lowers you, as it must,
into the foundation
of your grief counsellor's
new mansion.

The Bailiff's Daughter

after Austin Clarke

When the over-ripe haddock
Stirred in their stomachs
And the whiff brought the bluebottles in,
They say her voice
Was a Kate Bush song shrieked
By a cantankerous priest
With cancer in his throat
And many in the fluorescence
Thought her chin
Too sharp for its own good,
For the house of the bailiff
Is known by the nooses
Locals drape on its hedges
To remind them what's coming.

Men who had pictured her
During moments of intimacy
And found the thought of her face
A great way of slowing things down
Drank aftershave from tin cans
And loudly said nothing,
The women were sharpening
Kitchen knives wherever she went –
Like an alarm going off
In the middle of the night
Or a lie told so widely
It elbows out truth,
She was the bitter Wednesday evening
In every week
When your last toe nail went black
And came off in the bath
Just as the boys and girls of the Garda Síochána
Ever so gently bashed down the door.

Review of Non-Existent Poetry Collection

These poems are as engaging as the mobile phone
that kept ringing during the last ever
performance of *Waiting for Godot*
at the Albanian National Theatre,
before the building was demolished
to make way for the largest
multi-storey car park
in the Balkans.

This is a volume slim and radical
as a student rioting in favour of
privatisation.

Most of its similes were born
in University College Cork
and were never expected
to actually
leave the campus.

Its metaphors are edgy
as getting out of bed
especially to vote for
the UK Independence Party,
then going home to continue
twiddling yourself off
into an eggcup
over and over again.

The way the words
Michael Flatley across the page
displays the highly developed
sense of absurdity one might expect
of a poet who carries an eggcup
with him everywhere (always the same
eggcup) though,
so far as anyone knows,
he hasn't eaten
an egg since at least Thursday
July the ninth,
Nineteen Ninety Five.

These line breaks are agile
as a Masters student
forever threatening to pleasure
his or her professor,
but never actually doing so.

The Captive Butt

after Czeslaw Milosz

When an approved committee of three PhDs in
Creative Writing, English and Political Science
have spent the required laboratory weeks
ensconced with your every thought, word, deed –
and found nothing of consequence –
your buttocks will be authorised
for a Literature Foundation supported
tour of the bigger bits of the United States.

Sometimes both cheeks together,
on discussion panels:
Can Poets Be Bought?
And who'd want one anyway?
co-Chaired by the cadavers
of five Professors of Comparative Literature
at Johns Hopkins or Stanford.

Other times each going their separate way –
gluteus maximus number one
whimpering out
its latest free verse tribute to itself
to rapt dozens
up and down the eastern seaboard –
part town crier, part infant in need of winding –

while its equal and opposite,
if slightly more pimpled, twin
talks its way in and out of the Celtic
Studies Departments of every University
from Vancouver to Caltech
on the topic *How contemporary Irish*
literature is putting the I back into Irish,
to the orgasmic applause of students
named Erin and Megan
forced to attend for credit.

On The Appointment of Director of Failed Bank To Executive Board of Literature Ireland

for Jonathan Sugarman

My Dear Writers & Readers,

Adhering to recent Arts Council guidelines,
we are adjusting
our corporate governance structures
to include more criminal psychopaths
and people who just don't know what they're doing
per capita than are allowed exist
wherever the average eejit gathers
to do his or her thing.

To this end, and furthermore, to help me,
I mean 'us', avail of the expertise
of those with experience running the real economy,
I am appointing to my board a man
with a wide-brimmed felt hat
who has supplied political and business
conferences down and up the country
with all levels of women.

To assist in the enforcement area
we are anointing a bloke who for our purposes
will go by the name "Anto";
who may have unexplained income
about which the Criminal Assets Bureau
would love to have a chat
but that is none of my business or,
if you know what's good for you, yours.

Finally, from next month
the skeleton of a different one
of David Lloyd George's mistresses
will sit in on each of our meetings
to advise on social agility.

Yours transparently,

Chief Administrator,
Literature Ireland

The Caint* World Festival
of Literary Intercourse

This year's highlight: the alleged papist,
who denies everything (and more besides)
in conflagration with the retired pederast,
who was never exactly convicted of anything,
on the rickety main stage,
where so many of the greatest drawers down
of state aid in the history of literature
have of late been paraded. In the chair,
for what's hoped will be a wide ranging
and, at times, violent discussion
Professor Malcolm McArthur
of the University of Tullamore –
International Studies Department.
Each attendee is advised to bring
his or her own lump hammer.

To help keep your eyes ajar during
our more catastrophically dull events
we advise festival attendees not lucky enough to find
a sympathetic brothel to sob the afternoon away in,
to start taking odds, which emerging poet of which gender
will spend the night bouncing
up and down on the withered novelist
from Coupon, Pennsylvania.

Later, you can retire to our festival club;
watch a guy who seems to think you know who he is,
have a whiskey induced fit of roaring
about train strikes and how we need to get back
to James Joyce (the books, not the railway station
named after him). Or ask a woman you thought
might be Lionel Shriver the time
and realise when she looks at you as if
you'd just dipped your penis or,
if you're a woman, the nearest available penis
in her Long Island Iced Tea;

that she is in fact Literary Correspondent
of The Dawkey Episcopalian,
and didn't get where she isn't today
by telling the likes of you the time.

* "Caint" is Gaelic for talk. In days of yore school teachers would often shout
at the children in their charge "Na bí ag caint" (Don't be talking) and then
beat them savagely with bamboo sticks about the hands if they disobeyed.

Grasp

in memoriam poet of page & stage Eiléan Ní Faitíos

grasp at roses growing happily
red in other people's gardens
snip off every last fucking one of them
with the hedge clippers
you use to clear a path through the forest
on your lover's back

drive laughing through the streets
texting minor celebrities
whose phones all allegedly died
in Adam Clayton's former bidet

grasp the golf stick
and learn to beat in
heads no longer of use to you

wake the opportunists
who'd re-Tweet anything
jaysus do
some say *let them stew*
in piss pots of their own making
each of them a cross between
a chimpanzee and a yeast infection
but they're your chimpanzees

grasp the corpse of Eva Gore Booth
and go about the place in a people carrier
owning it   dump your agent
your auctioneer
        your orthodontist
they are not worthy

grasp that microphone and shout out
how one night
you tore the big wet lips off her
and made them your own

tell them grasp the pipe and blow
white smoke up all the right holes

given the chance
to do the necessary
grasp it   both hands
and talk so fast no one notices they're dead

After The Revolution

for and entirely inspired by Quincy Lehr

We will pay homeless people to follow
poet and critic Matthias Wetruder. And not just
into drug-stores, dry-cleaners, and taxi-cabs
(though there too) but also into Japanese restaurants
where said homeless person will sit
next table vociferously demanding,
as will be his or her right,
tomato ketchup with their sushi;

into seminars at first NYU,
then the University of Houston, on *Uselessness
in The Work of Matthias Wetruder*
where they'll angrily ask questions about Matthias
that Matthias can't answer; around

branches of Barnes & Noble wearing
a coat with a fungal infection
(and no belt) reciting from the latest
translation into Albanian of Sophocles;

into performances of *Vespers for a New Dark Age*
at the New York Metropolitan Opera
where they'll sit behind Matthias making it clear,
by their very body odour,
they know what he's up to;

around award ceremonies where
Matthias Wetruder is due to present an award
to Matthias Wetruder; and most of all into

men's rooms where they'll loiter
in the neighbouring cubicle
loudly eating the yoghurt
we'll pay people like them to eat
in men's rooms after the revolution.

The Crowning of the Prophet Una

"A PR disaster coupled with an angry public and small local protests are distracting from the topic of water security."

UNA MULLALLY, *Why We Should Pay for Water*, Irish Times, May 12th, 2014

"Media appears unable to interpret political movements formed outside traditional party structures."

UNA MULLALLY, *Why are Irish journalists again missing a movement?*, Irish Times, Aprll 16th, 2018

Her weekly commandments we caw in unison
from our twin mountaintops: Twitbark and Facepalm.

She's this millennium's equivalent of an old-style Archbishop
and we'd happily wrestle for the privilege

of placing, with our trembly fingers,
a diamond studded mitre

on her frail skull. It's said
to renew her cred

each week she has a black woman
or a gypsy for dinner — as a guest

and not as part of the meal
as most of her journalistic colleagues

prefer. When her predictions come true
we run through the streets screaming

our big watery eyed yes!
Carve her words in glorifying marble

until our pale clappers bleed like Padre Pio's.
When they turn out to be what rhymes with

farce, we dutifully delete them from our heads
and, where we can, the heads of others

making liberal use of the purifying hacksaw we get free
with Monday's *Times*; keep our minds pristine

as a scrap of paper with print on it so small
only busybody cranks and half dead Bolsheviks
with issues feel the need to read it.

Among Savages

I'm secretly posh and I'm protestant
and no one believes the accent I got
off a man in Stoneybatter is real.

My dad earned the Krugerrands,
with which I paid for this house,
flogging rockets to
good-old-days South Africa.
My given name, Giles Amery the Eighth,
sounds great when you say it in Gaelic.

Each night I arrive at some party
to which I wasn't invited,
carrying half a banjo
and sing songs made up of
things Brendan Behan
never actually said.

A small unsalted tear tumbles into
my half pint of alcohol-free Guinness,
every time I think of the boys from the estate
beyond the two big fields
behind the high, high wall we built
to keep them out;

how afraid I still am
they'll one day
hold me down and make me talk
posh and protestant,
because even when it's accompanied
with the bit of a beard I borrowed
from Ronnie Drew,

they know the accent I got
off that man in Stoneybatter
isn't mine to speak.

Treatise on Uselessness

Throughout my truly enormous life,
I've never found a use for
gypsies.

When one decides to spend the night
searching online
for a worse deal
on one's house insurance,
there's never
a gypsy about to help.

Or when one advertises a vacancy
for Associate Professor of English at Trinity
there's hardly ever a gypsy
around to fill it.

Or when the wedding
of an Eritrean goatherd and his beloved
is in crying need of a cruise missile,
there's never a gypsy available
to press the required buttons
and later tell the inquiry
it was all a terrible
misunderstanding.

Despite millions ingested
by social programmes, we've mostly
failed to submerge gypsies
in the internationally agreed system
of an indecent day's pay
for a decent week's work.

Yet the state insists
on making gypsies compulsory
for those who'd rather never
have to speak to one.

What practical purpose does it serve
for us to continue to try to absorb
gypsies into what my late Popsicle
— a one time Viceroy of Upper Munster — used to call
society,

when all but a few fanatics know it's futile
as trying to teach a Latvian cage dancer
how to speak Irish?

Acknowledgments

Acknowledgments are due to the following magazines, newspapers and anthologies in which versions of some of these poems first appeared: *The Moth, The Stinging Fly, The Irish Times* (online), *Hot Press, The North* (UK), *The Raintown Review* (USA), *Broadsheet.ie, Rabble.ie, ROPES, Skylight 47, Crannóg, Headstuff, The Bangor Literary Journal, North West Words, The Bogman's Cannon, The Galway Advertiser, GalwayDaily.com, Anomaly Literary Magazine* (U.K.), *Poethead* (Ed. Chris Murray), *The Pileus* (UK), *The Platform* (UK), *Reknr* (UK), *Red Poets* (UK), *Socialist Unity* (Ed. Andy Newman), *Scum Gentry – Alternative Arts & Media, Culture Matters* (Ed. Mike Quille), *The Morning Star* (U.K.), *Labour Against The Witch Hunt* website (UK), *The Weekly Worker* (UK), Clare Daly TD's Facebook page, *Poetry & All That Jazz* (Chichester Poetry Festival), *Poems on The Edge, Live Encounters – Poetry & Writing, Poetica Review* (UK), *Poets Speak – Survival* (New Mexico), *Manzano Mountain Review* (New Mexico), *Colors Magazine* (Montana), *Facts For Working People* (USA), *The Ofi Press* (Mexico), *Light Journal* (USA), and *Poems for Grenfell Tower* (The Onslaught Press).

'Sarcoid Years' was broadcast on RTE Lyric FM's Poetry File, an extract from 'What Did The Politician Get His Wife' was read aloud by film director Ken Loach at a Labour Against The Witchunt meeting in London in January 2018, and 'Anatomy of a Bomb Scare' was broadcast by Jacqueline Walker on her Youtube channel in September 2018.

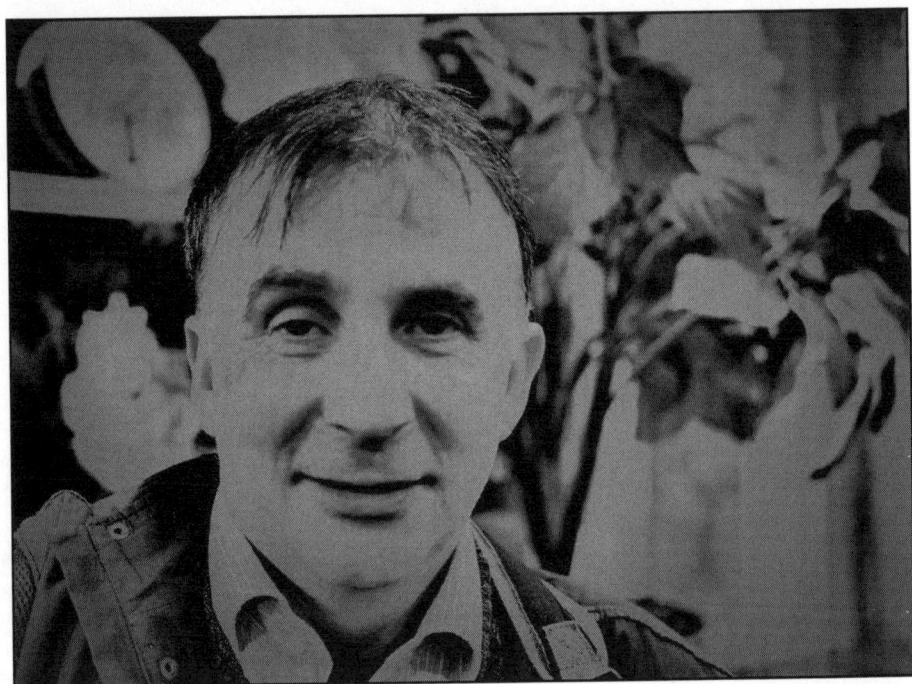

KEVIN HIGGINS is co-organiser of Over The Edge literary events in Galway, Ireland. He teaches poetry workshops at Galway Arts Centre, Creative Writing at Galway Technical Institute, and is Creative Writing Director for the National University of Ireland – Galway Summer School. He is poetry critic of *The Galway Advertiser*. His poetry is discussed in *The Cambridge Introduction to Modern Irish Poetry* and features in the generation defining anthology *Identity Parade – New British and Irish Poets* (Ed. Roddy Lumsden, Bloodaxe, 2010) and in *The Hundred Years' War: modern war poems* (Ed. Neil Astley, Bloodaxe, April 2014). Kevin's poetry has been translated into Greek, Spanish, Italian, Japanese, German, Serbian, Russian, & Portuguese. In 2014 Kevin's poetry was the subject of a paper 'The Case of Kevin Higgins, or, The Present State of Irish Poetic Satire' presented by David Wheatley at a Symposium on Satire at the University of Aberdeen. He was Satirist-in-Residence at the Bogman's Cannon (2015-16). *2016 – The Selected Satires of Kevin Higgins* was published by NuaScéalta in 2016; a pamphlet of Kevin's political poems *The Minister For Poetry Has Decreed* was published, also in 2016, by the Culture Matters imprint of the UK based Manifesto Press. His poems have been praised by, among others, Tony Blair's biographer John Rentoul, *Observer* columnist Nick Cohen, historian Ruth Dudley Edwards, and *Sunday Independent* columnist Gene Kerrigan; have been quoted in *The Daily Telegraph*, *The Times* (UK), *The Independent*, *The Daily Mirror*, *Hot Press* magazine and on *Tonight With Vincent Browne*; and read aloud by the film director Ken Loach at a political meeting in London. In 2016 *The Stinging Fly* magazine described Kevin as "likely the most read living poet in Ireland." He has published five collections of poetry with Salmon, most recently *Song of Songs 2.0: New & Selected Poems* (2017). Kevin has read his work at Arts Council and Culture Ireland supported poetry events in Kansas City, USA (2006), Los Angeles, USA (2007), London, UK (2007), New York, USA (2008), Athens, Greece (2008); St. Louis, USA (2008), Chicago, USA (2009), Denver, USA (2010), Washington D.C (2011), Huntington, West Virginia, USA (2011), Geelong, Australia (2011), Canberra, Australia (2011), St. Louis, USA (2013), Boston, Massachusetts, USA (2013) & Amherst, Massachusetts, USA (2013), & New Mexico, USA (2018). *Sex and Death at Merlin Park Hospital* is his fifth full collection of poems.

salmonpoetry

Cliffs of Moher, County Clare, Ireland

"Like the sea-run Steelhead salmon that thrashes upstream to its spawning ground, then instead of dying, returns to the sea – Salmon Poetry Press brings precious cargo to both Ireland and America in the poetry it publishes, then carries that select work to its readership against incalculable odds."

TESS GALLAGHER

The Salmon Bookshop
& Literary Centre
Ennistymon, County Clare, Ireland